Twilight Zone

John Woodward

Heinemann Library
Chicago, Illinois

Consultant: Lundie Spence, PhD
Director, SouthEast Center for Ocean Sciences Education Excellence, South Carolina Sea Grant Consortium

Produced by The Brown Reference Group plc
Project Editor: Tim Harris
Sub Editor: Tom Webber
Designer: Jeni Child
Picture Researcher: Sean Hannaway
Illustrator: Mark Walker
Managing Editor: Bridget Giles

Printed in China by WKT Company Limited

08 07 06 05 04
10 9 8 7 6 5 4 3 2 1

Library of Congress Cataloging-in-Publication data

Woodward, John, 1954-
  Twilight zone / John Woodward.
     v. cm. -- (Exploring the oceans)
Includes bibliographical references and index.
Contents: The blue twilight -- Your mission -- Fishing the depths -- Dawn descent -- Getting darker -- Getting colder -- Coming up -- Microscopic life -- Marine snow -- A deep-sea vampire squid -- The deep scattering layer -- Rise and fall -- Big-eyed hunters -- Top predators -- Mirrors and light -- Deepwater giants -- Talking whales -- Heading south -- Deep currents -- Diving with elephant seals -- Mission debriefing.
  ISBN 1-4034-5129-X (hardcover) -- ISBN 1-4034-5135-4 (pbk.)
 1. Oceanography--Juvenile literature. 2. Deep-sea sounding--Juvenile literature. 3. Deep-sea animals--Juvenile literature. [1. Oceanography. 2. Deep-sea ecology. 3. Ecology.] I. Title.
  GC21.5.W66 2004
  551.46--dc22

                                    2003021292

Acknowledgements
The author and publishers are grateful to the following for permission to reproduce copyright material:
Front Cover: Mesopelagic squid in the Atlantic Ocean (David Shale/Nature Picture Library).
Back Cover: Mark A. Johnson/Corbis
p.1 Peter David/Natural Visions; p.2t Heather Angel/Natural Visions; p.2c Chris McLaughlin/Corbis; p.2b Amos Nachoum/Corbis; p.3 Francois Gohier/Ardea; p.4–5 Frank & Joyce Burek/Photodisc, Inc; p.7 Kim Westerskov/Oxford Scientific Films; p.8–9 Amos Nachoum/Corbis; p.10b Norbert Wu/NHPA; p.10–11 Anne Norris/Natural Visions; p.11 Norbert Wu/NHPA; p.12 Oxford Scientific Films; p.13t Ralph White/Corbis; p.13b Heather Angel/Natural Visions; p.14 Heather Angel/Natural Visions; p.15 NOAA; p.16-17 Jonathan Blair/Corbis; p.18 Stuart Donachie/Ecoscene; p.18–19 Peter David/Natural Visions; p.20–21 Heather Angel/Natural Visions; p.21 Heather Angel/Natural Visions; p.22 Kim Reisenbichler/MBARI; p.22–23 Chris McLaughlin/Corbis; p.25 Adrian Davies/Nature Picture Library; p.25b Ralph White/Corbis; p.26b Rudie Kuiter/Oxford Scientific Films; p.26–27 Heather Angel/Natural Visions; p.28–29 Peter David/Natural Visions; p.29b Norbert Wu/Oxford Scientific Films; p.30-31 Corbis Royalty Free; p.32 Heather Angel/Natural Visions; p.33 Peter Herring/Natural Visions; p.35 Thomas Haider/Oxford Scientific Films; p.36b Iain Kerr/Ocean Alliance; p.36–37 Francois Gohier/Ardea; p.38b NOAA; p.38–39 Heather Angel/Natural Visions; p.39t Rich Kirchner/NHPA; p.40–41 Ian McDonald/NOAA; p.42–43 Doc White/Nature Picture Library; p.44 Heather Angel/Natural Visions.

Some words are shown in bold, **like this.** You can find out what they mean by looking in the glossary.

Contents

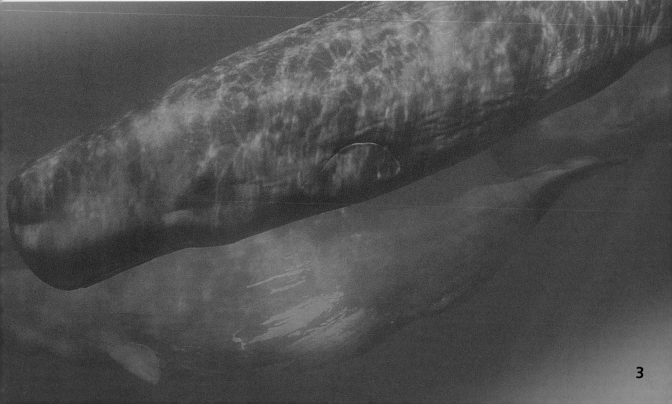

The Blue Twilight

More than two-thirds of our planet is covered by the oceans. Each ocean is a vast area of water that takes days or even weeks to cross by boat. When you are in the middle of an ocean, you can see nothing but water and sky.

A long way down

But the oceans are not just wide. They are very deep, too. If you dropped a stone over the side of a boat in midocean, it would sink through at least 11,500 feet (3,500 meters) of water before settling on the ocean floor. That is more than 2 miles (3 kilometers) deep. The stone would pass through the sunlit surface layer quickly, because the sunlit zone is 600 feet (180 meters) deep at most. Then it would sink into water where there is hardly any light at all, except a faint blue glow. This is the twilight zone. Eventually, the stone would sink into very deep water that is completely dark. This is the midnight zone.

Only a few people have explored the deepest, darkest parts of the oceans. The ocean depths are too deep for divers wearing **scuba** gear. To find out more about the deep oceans, we need small submarines called **submersibles.** Submersibles are designed to protect us from the cold and the **water pressure.** We need powerful lights to see through the darkness. And we need special equipment for gathering scientific data.

Your mission is to dive through the twilight zone. There you will search for signs of life and see how the dark ocean differs from the sunlit zone.

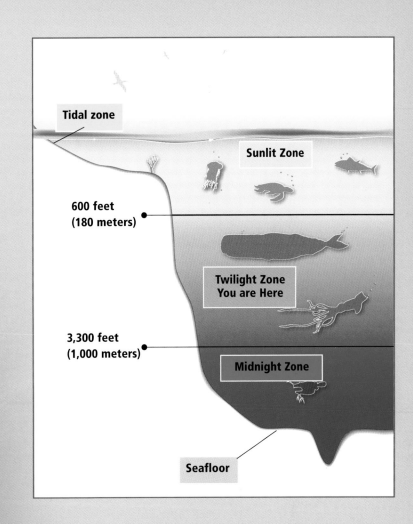

Tidal zone

Sunlit Zone

600 feet
(180 meters)

Twilight Zone
You are Here

3,300 feet
(1,000 meters)

Midnight Zone

Seafloor

*On your way down through
the sunlit zone, you might
catch sight of a large,
graceful manta ray.*

Your Mission

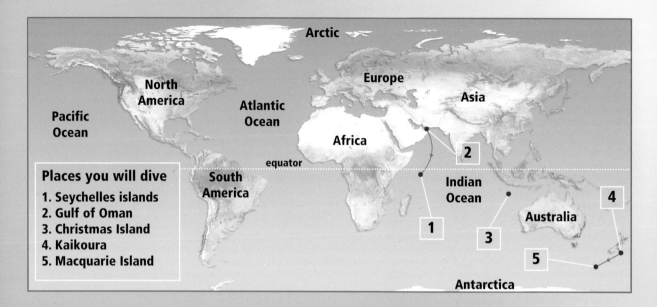

Arctic

Europe

Asia

North
America

Atlantic
Ocean

Pacific
Ocean

Africa

2

equator

Places you will dive

South
America

1. Seychelles islands
2. Gulf of Oman
3. Christmas Island
4. Kaikoura
5. Macquarie Island

Indian
Ocean

4

1

Australia

3

5

Antarctica

Ocean water **absorbs** sunlight. Near the surface, you cannot really see this. But as you go deeper, more and more of the light is absorbed. The water slowly changes color and slowly gets darker. Sunlight includes all the colors of the rainbow, but the water absorbs the red light first, then the yellow, and then the green. At 330 feet (100 meters) below the surface, there is only blue light left. That makes the water look blue.

In a clear, **tropical** ocean there is still some blue light at this depth. It is like looking through a sheet of blue-tinted glass. But as you go even deeper, the light slowly fades. At 600 feet (180 meters), which is the beginning of the twilight zone, there is still a little bit of light. However, it is barely enough to see by. The ocean only becomes completely dark at about 3,300 feet (1,000 meters), where the midnight zone begins.

Water pressure

On your travels in the twilight zone, you will use several submersibles. Each one needs to be very strong. Otherwise, the huge weight of water above the submersible would crush it flat. When scientists dive to great depths, they sometimes tie styrofoam drinking cups to the outside of their submersible. When they get back to the surface, the cups have been crushed to the size of thimbles by the **water pressure.**

Going down

You are going to find out what happens in the twilight zone. Your mission starts off the Seychelles, a group of islands in the Indian Ocean. There, you will discover just what it is like to go down into the blue twilight. You will see how ocean life changes as you go deeper.

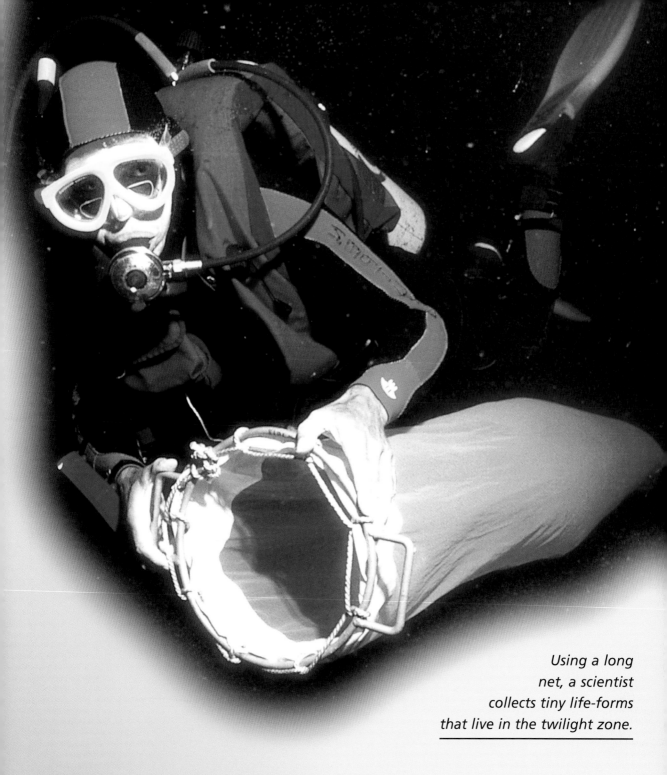

Using a long net, a scientist collects tiny life-forms that live in the twilight zone.

You will use scientific equipment to make discoveries in the twilight zone. Your adventure starts in the northern Indian Ocean. Then, your journey will take you southeast around the Indian Ocean to the deep waters off southern Australia. There, you will meet with some of the hunters, or **predators,** that patrol the deep ocean in search of **prey.** Some of the predators look unlike any you have seen before.

Finally, you will explore an ocean **current.** You will find out how currents affect life in the oceans and even on land.

Fishing the Depths

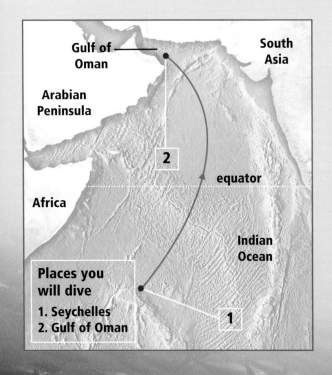

Gulf of Oman

South Asia

Arabian Peninsula

equator

Africa

Indian Ocean

Places you will dive
1. Seychelles
2. Gulf of Oman

You are going to find out more about the twilight zone near the beautiful Seychelles islands. They lie in the western Indian Ocean, not far from the **equator.** The islands are the tops of huge underwater mountains that rise from the ocean floor. Although the ocean water is shallow near the shore, it soon gets very, very deep. From the air, the islands and the shallow waters around them look like green and turquoise jewels in a vast, deep blue ocean.

You join some local fishers on a boat that is going on a fishing trip. The fishers have nets that are long enough to reach down

into the twilight zone. You want to know what lives in the twilight zone. Looking at what the fishers haul up in their nets seems a good way to find out.

The boat leaves the harbor and makes its way through a **coral reef** toward the ocean. The water is crystal clear. You can see the seafloor clearly in the shallows. But beyond the reef, you can see nothing at all through the dark blue water. Now you know you are over the deep ocean. The fishers set their nets, and you wait.

You have asked the fishers to set one net near the surface and another much deeper. You want to see if they catch different kinds of fish at different depths. The deep net takes longer to let out and haul in, so you haul in the shallow net first. It has caught a lot of fish. Most are small, **streamlined** fish that swim in groups or schools. There are also a few

tuna. They can swim quickly and catch other fish to eat. All of the fish caught in the first net live in the sunlit zone.

A different world

When the fishers haul in the deeper net, one thing is obvious: there are far fewer fish. And the fish look very strange. Many are flattened and silvery. They are smaller than the fish from the sunlit zone, yet many have big mouths with long, needlelike teeth. There are also small squid with big eyes and weird creatures made of see-through jelly.

The fishers throw most of these strange creatures back into the ocean, since they are no use to them. But you have learned something from the **organisms.** The twilight zone is a different world.

A group, or school, of tuna fish swims through the sunlit zone in search of food.

Dawn Descent

You decide to take a trip down to the twilight zone yourself, to see what it is like. A trip like this is expensive. You need a **submersible** and a **mother ship.** The mother ship will lower the submersible into the water and haul it out again. You also need a crew who know what they are doing. Your life may depend on them if something goes wrong.

You can certainly depend on the crew of the research ship *Thetis,* which is working near a **coral reef** in the Seychelles islands. The ship is equipped with a one-person mini-submersible that can go down to 2,300 feet (700 meters). That will be deep enough. You have already set up the dive. By the time you arrive at dawn, the submersible is ready. You climb in and lock down the thick, see-through plastic dome. The crew lower you over the side, and down you go.

As the submersible goes deeper, you leave behind the animals that live in the sunlit zone like this green turtle (right). You then see a blue shark (below). It spends some of its time in the twilight zone.

A submersible (right) has a clear window and powerful lights. These features help the crew see what is in dark water.

The sunlit ocean

Before you reach the depths of the twilight zone, you must pass through the sunlit zone near the surface. At first, the view is breathtaking. Shoals of brilliantly colored fish swim past, and a sleek gray shark glides by. You can see a long way through the water because there is very little **plankton.** Plankton are tiny, drifting animals and plantlike **algae** that often make the water cloudy.

The algae in the plankton make sugar and other foods. They use the energy of sunlight to make sugars from water and carbon dioxide gas **dissolved** in the water. This is called **photosynthesis.** The algae are the main source of food in the sunlit zone of the ocean. So, cloudy ocean water with a lot of plankton is much richer in food than clear water. But even clear water has some plankton. This is eaten by all kinds of animals from shrimp and small fish to giant whales.

Getting Darker

As your **submersible** sinks deeper, its instruments tell you that you are more than 600 feet (180 meters) beneath the surface. You are in the twilight zone. The mechanical arm of your submersible looks dark blue in the dim light, and although the water is clear you cannot see much else.

You switch on the submersible's lights. They shine out through the water, picking out small fish that reflect the light like mirrors. There are other things in the water, too. A weird object that looks like a see-through pumpkin drifts by. It flashes with rainbow colors. It is a comb jelly, which drives itself through the water with rippling rows of moving "combs." The combs **reflect** and scatter light, creating the rainbow effect.

A delicate comb jelly (below) shines rainbow colors as your submersible passes.

You can see tiny flecks in the water that might be small floating animals, but you would need a **microscope** to check. You make a note to sample the plankton when you have finished the dive. Then another peculiar animal appears. It looks like a see-through slug. But it is using a pair of winglike fins to push itself along. It is a sea butterfly.

A light show

The sea butterfly swims slowly away, out of the area that is lit up by the submersible's lights. You are about to turn the submersible to follow it, when something else attracts your attention. It is another light. The light is very faint, so you switch off the submersible's lights to check. You have not made a mistake. There is another light, and it is coming from a fish. No one is sure what kind of fish it is. It comes closer, and you can see rows of glowing blue lights on the fish's belly. Why would a fish light itself up like this? You find out the answer later on your adventure through the twilight zone. You watch, fascinated, as the fish swims over the submersible and away into the gloom.

Sea butterflies (right) are usually very small. Most grow only to around 2 inches (4 centimeters) long. They are named for their "wings."

Mini-submersible

The submersible you use for this dive is just big enough for one person. It is tube shaped and made of steel. It has a transparent dome on top made of tough plastic. The submersible is attached to the **mother ship** by a strong metal cable. The cable makes sure you do not drift away. The cable also supplies power for the lights, the propellers that drive the submersible through the water, and the mechanical arms that collect samples.

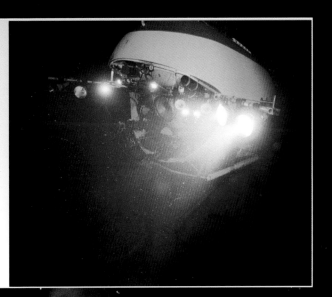

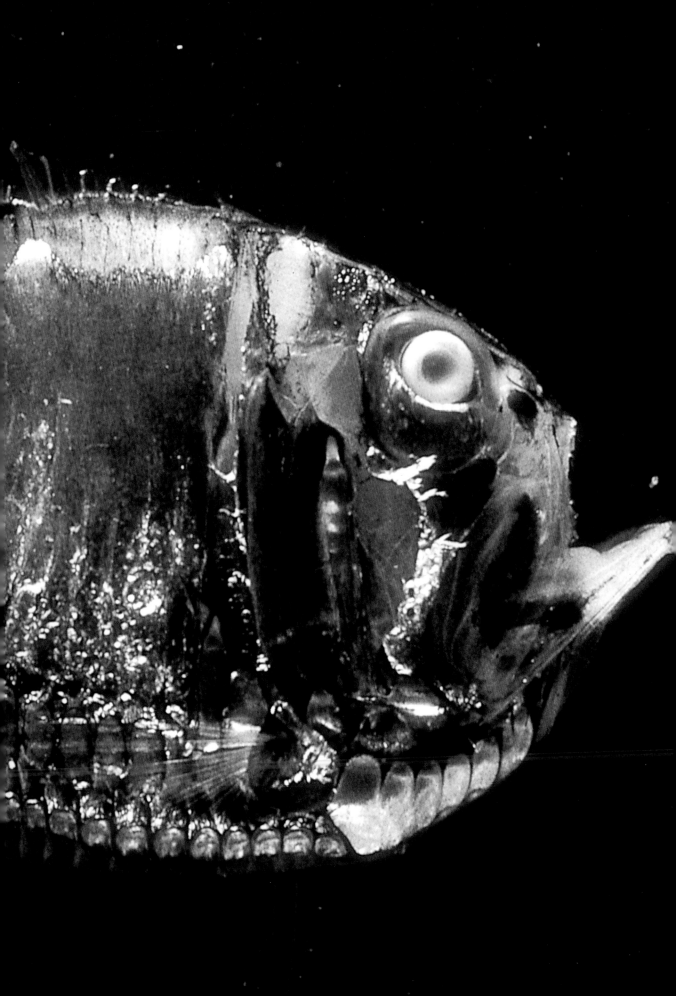

Getting Colder

Your **submersible** has such good **insulation** against the cold that you do not notice a dramatic change in the water temperature. Up at the ocean surface, the water is a comfortably warm 70 °F (21 °C), but 1,000 feet (300 meters) below the surface your temperature probe shows a chilly 45 °F (7 °C).

You have decided that this is as deep as you are going to go today. You ask the crew of the **mother ship** to start raising your submersible toward the surface. As you go up, the temperature probe shows the rising water temperature.

You expect the temperature to rise steadily as you get nearer the surface, but it is not exactly like that. The temperature certainly goes up, but in steps. The miniature screen of the submersible's computer shows a temperature change near the top of the twilight zone. At about 800 feet (240 meters), it starts rising much faster. Between there and around 600 feet (180 meters), it warms from 41 °F (5 °C) to 52 °F (11 °C). Then the rate of increase slows down again. The water is still getting warmer as you head for the surface, but not as quickly. The layer of water where the temperature rises quickly as you pass up through it is called a **thermocline.** As you pass down through it, the water gets colder very quickly.

Hatchet fish like this one are at home in the cold waters of the twilight zone.

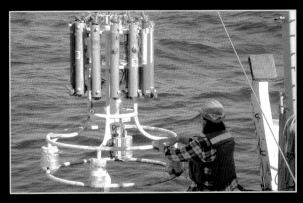

Your submersible is fitted with instruments like these. Some measure temperature, and others the ocean's chemical makeup.

Invisible wall

While the sensors have been recording the temperature, you have been looking at the creatures in the water. As the submersible passes through the thermocline, the animals change. There are different types of fish, comb jellies, and other animals. The thermocline seems to act like an invisible wall. It keeps most animals from moving from the twilight zone to the sunlit zone—or in the other direction.

The thermocline is very sudden in the centers of **tropical** oceans. Because the sun shines down all year, the sunlit zone stays warm all year in tropical places. Warm water is not as heavy as cold water. So a layer of warm water floats on top of the colder, deeper water. Nutrients are scarce in the top layer because they are used up by the algae. So, the water has little **plankton.** This is why tropical ocean waters are so clear.

Coming Up

You might think that diving in the twilight zone is a simple business. It is if you can go in a **submersible.** The crew of the **mother ship** lowers the heavy submersible over the side and lifts it out of the water again with powerful machinery. Then you undo the hatch and step out. What could be simpler?

Under pressure

But without a submersible, a diver who tried to dive very deep would soon be in big trouble. The air we breathe is a mixture of gases, including the oxygen that our bodies need. But most of the air is made up of a gas called nitrogen. Normally, the nitrogen is no problem. But, that changes if a diver goes much deeper than about 100 feet (30 meters) using cylinders of **compressed air.** Then, the **water pressure** makes the nitrogen do strange things. It gets into the diver's blood and fat, and if it gets to the brain it can cause a weird condition called **nitrogen narcosis.**

Divers who go too deep can be "drugged" by the nitrogen in their bodies. They think more slowly, and they get confused and clumsy. This can be very dangerous, because if divers are confused they can lose track of what they are doing. They may even drown. Luckily, returning to shallower water cures the problem, as long as the diver comes up slowly.

These divers have been collecting samples. They have to take care not to go too deep or return to the surface too fast. If they do, they can become very ill.

Deadly bubbles

A human diver faces another problem when coming back to the surface. If he or she comes up too fast, the nitrogen makes bubbles in his or her blood. This causes a very painful condition called

the bends. It can even kill a diver. Most divers prevent this by coming up slowly, and even stopping for a while halfway up. But deep-sea divers have to spend hours or even days inside a **decompression chamber** while their bodies gradually get rid of the nitrogen.

And divers face another big problem. Without the protection of a submersible, someone diving in the twilight zone would be crushed by the **water pressure,** the weight of ocean water above him or her. It is impossible for people to explore the twilight zone without a submersible.

Microscopic Life

Scientists lower a large nylon net over the side of the ship. It will gather plankton for them to study.

When you check your catch, it is disappointing. It looks like gray sludge. You need to take it down to the ship's laboratory and put it under a **microscope** to see what is really there.

A glittering haul

The microscope magnifies the sludge to 20 times its real size. You see a glittering array of tiny, see-through creatures. Most of them are crustaceans of some kind. Crustaceans are insectlike animals with armored bodies and jointed legs. Big crustaceans include the heavy crabs and lobsters that crawl over the seafloor. But those you have caught are tiny.

When you add some of the sludge to seawater, you can see how the crustaceans hang in the water using long spines and hairs like parachutes. They can also swim by twitching their tiny legs. Some look like the shrimp that live in coastal tidepools, and others look a bit like fleas. But most of them are T-shaped creatures with long **antennae** forming the top of the "T." They are copepods.

More than two-thirds of the animals in the ocean plankton are copepods.

Back on board, you remember seeing tiny flecks in the water. They were lit up by the **submersible's** lights like dust in a sunbeam. You need to catch some to find out what they are. To do this you use a nylon net with a very fine mesh. It is designed to trap small **plankton.** The mouth of the net can be opened and shut. You can lower the net to 1,000 feet (300 meters), open it, then shut it again. This makes sure that everything in the net has come from the twilight zone and not from the sunlit zone.

There are probably more copepods on Earth than any other type of animal. In the sunlit zone, copepods feed on planktonic algae. There, copepods scoop the **algae** from the water with their swimming legs.

You have already found out that algae cannot survive in the twilight zone because there is not enough light for them to make food. So what do the copepods eat? That is the next puzzle to figure out.

Copepods are very small. You need to look at them through a microscope to get a better view of what they look like.

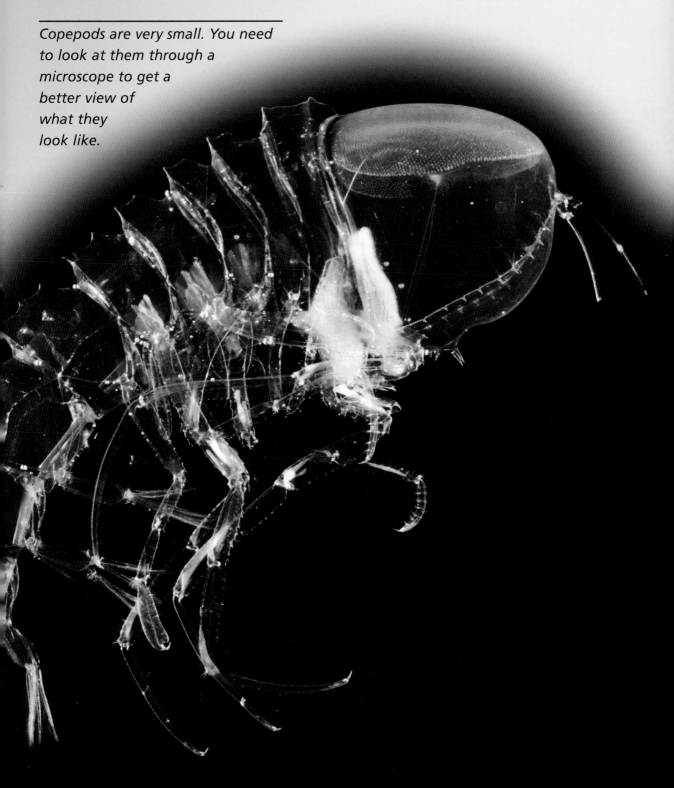

Marine Snow

As you use your **microscope** to watch the tiny crustaceans moving through the water, you notice something else. There are even smaller objects drifting between them. To get a better view, you take a small sample of the water and slip it under a more powerful microscope. This can make things look 1,000 times bigger than they really are.

Many of the smaller objects are tiny fragments of dead **algae** and dead animals. You can see broken pieces of shell and bits of spines and legs. They are all that is left of **plankton** that has been attacked by other animals, or has simply died. There are also other things that are just lumps of solid matter. They turn out to be the **feces** of fish and other animals.

These bits are the remains of living things, or organisms, so they are **organic.** Organic material is made of substances that other animals may be able to use as food. Many small animals are experts at clearing up organic junk, and they eat nothing else. On land, they live in the soil and eat things like dead leaves. In the ocean, most junk eaters live in the twilight zone and below.

Nearly all the organic debris has come from near the ocean surface, in the sunlit zone. It has slowly sunk downward, like

Powerful microscope

You have been using a powerful **microscope** that can **magnify** objects to 1,000 times their real size. It can also work at lower magnification, if you switch to a different lens. So, you can start off at low power, then zoom in close on something like this copepod.

snow falling through the air. The junk is often called marine snow. If nothing eats it, the marine snow keeps sinking until it reaches the seafloor.

The copepods and other animals that you have brought up from the twilight zone have all been feeding on marine snow. This explains how they can survive in a place where there is not enough light for algae to make food through **photosynthesis.** The copepods are eaten by other animals, and these animals are eaten by even bigger hunters. The marine snow supports a whole deepwater **food chain.**

This water sample has been magnified by a microscope. The shrimplike things are copepods. The tiny bits are marine snow.

A Deep-Sea Vampire Squid

The research ship *Thetis* is heading north from the Seychelles to the Gulf of Oman, between Arabia and India. It is going there to investigate a strange feature of the ocean called the **oxygen minimum layer.** You decide to go, too.

Oxygen is the gas that all living things use to make energy out of food. On land, we get it from the air we breathe. But oxygen is also **dissolved** in the water of the ocean. Marine animals can absorb it into their bodies through their skin or **gills.**

Cold water holds more dissolved oxygen than warm water. There is also plenty of dissolved oxygen near the ocean surface because it is close to the air. There is a layer of water near

A vampire squid's eyes glow blue when a submersible's lights shine on them.

the bottom of the twilight zone that contains less dissolved oxygen than the water above or below it. This layer traps **organic** junk or marine snow, and bacteria **decompose** the junk. As they do, the bacteria use up oxygen in the water. This layer is called the oxygen minimum layer. It lies about 2,000–2,600 feet (600–800 meters) below the surface of the ocean.

The effect of this layer varies from place to place. It is very strong in the Gulf of Oman. Oxygen probes lowered from the ship show that there is about 20 times less oxygen than there is in air at the surface. Not many animals can survive living in water with so little oxygen. So, the oxygen minimum layer acts like an invisible barrier in the ocean, keeping animals from moving up or down through it. You have already discovered another invisible barrier—the **thermocline** that you found near the Seychelles.

Luckily the layer is no barrier to your **submersible,** so you take the craft down to have a look. As you expected, there is not a lot to see when you get there. You keep looking, because you have heard about a strange animal that does live here. Then you see one: a vampire squid. It is very dark red, with eyes that glow blue in the submersible's lights. It is only about 8 inches (20 centimeters) long—that is as long as a school book—but it looks a bit scary.

The vampire squid has very big gills and unusual blood that is very good at **absorbing** oxygen. A vampire squid can spend its whole life in the oxygen minimum layer. It feeds on the few other animals that share its space.

Sitting in your submersible, you can watch and wait for signs of life in the twilight zone.

The Deep Scattering Layer

Place you will dive
1. Christmas Island

Sumatra

Borneo

Java

Indian Ocean

1

Australia

The ocean floor in this region is known to be more than 16,400 feet (5,000 meters) deep. But the screen seems to show two ocean floors. One is where it should be, but the other is in the twilight zone, around 1,300 feet (400 meters) below the surface. The scientists on board just ignore the shallower signal. They know that it is nothing to do with the seafloor. It is something completely different, called the **deep scattering layer.**

Layer of life

The *Capricorn* has a small **submersible** that works by remote control. It is called an **ROV,** or remotely operated vehicle. You sit in the control room at the surface, and use a lever to guide the vehicle as you watch a video screen. Someone tells you how to drive the ROV. Then it is an easy job to launch the ROV and drive it down to take a look at the deep scattering layer.

Y ou leave the *Thetis* working in the Gulf of Oman, and fly southeast to Christmas Island, south of Java. The island is the tip of an underwater mountain. The mountain rises about 20,000 feet (6,000 meters) from the floor of the Indian Ocean. Anchored just offshore is the Australian survey ship *Capricorn.* It is specially equipped for mapping the ocean floor. It uses a system called **sonar.**

You join the ship, which is heading south to work in the cooler water off Western Australia. When the crew starts surveying, you are invited to watch the computer screen that displays the results. It is soon clear that something strange is happening.

The water in the deep scattering layer is teeming with life. There are tiny animals like copepods and shrimp, and many bigger animals such as jellyfish and squid. You see a big red jellyfish that must be as long as a large dog. And there are masses of fish, all gleaming with weird light from rows of small light-producing **organs** on their bodies. The deep scattering layer is a great swarm of deep-ocean life.

There are many different life-forms in the deep scattering layer, both large and small.

Sonar

A **sonar** device fires pulses of sound down through the water from the submersible (right). When each signal hits the bottom it bounces back to the submersible. The longer the signal takes to do this, the deeper the water. A computer works out the depth, and shows the result on a screen.

Rise and Fall

As night falls, the scientists on board *Capricorn* keep their **sonar** equipment running. They have something to show you.

The **deep scattering layer** is now much shallower. It has moved higher in the water column and is less than 500 feet (150 meters) from the surface. So all the animals that you saw at 1,300 feet (400 meters) must have risen up through the water. The animals were in the twilight zone, but now they have moved into the sunlit zone.

Just to check, you launch the **ROV** to take a look. When you switch on the ROV's lamps in the deep scattering layer, they light up swarms of **plankton,** jellyfish, and fish that have all migrated toward the surface in the dark. For small animals like copepods, it is an amazing journey of 800 feet (240 meters). It takes them three hours or more. Fish can swim faster, but they might also come from farther down. Some lantern fish—the ones with glowing lights—may even come from beyond the twilight zone. Some rise from more than 5,000 feet (1,500 meters) below the waves.

As you steer the ROV, the clouds in the night sky far above you drift away to reveal a bright full moon. Soon, the animals start to move down through the water. You have to move the ROV down to keep track of them. They obviously do not like the moonlight, but why not? And why did they come to the surface in the first place?

Microscopic feast

Since the swarms of animals are near the surface, you decide to catch some of the smaller ones so you can check them out. When you look at them under the **microscope,** you discover a whole mass of even smaller plankton. They are **algae,** the plantlike organisms that make food by **photosynthesis** using the energy of sunlight.

This fish lives in the twilight zone during the day. At night it rises into shallower water.

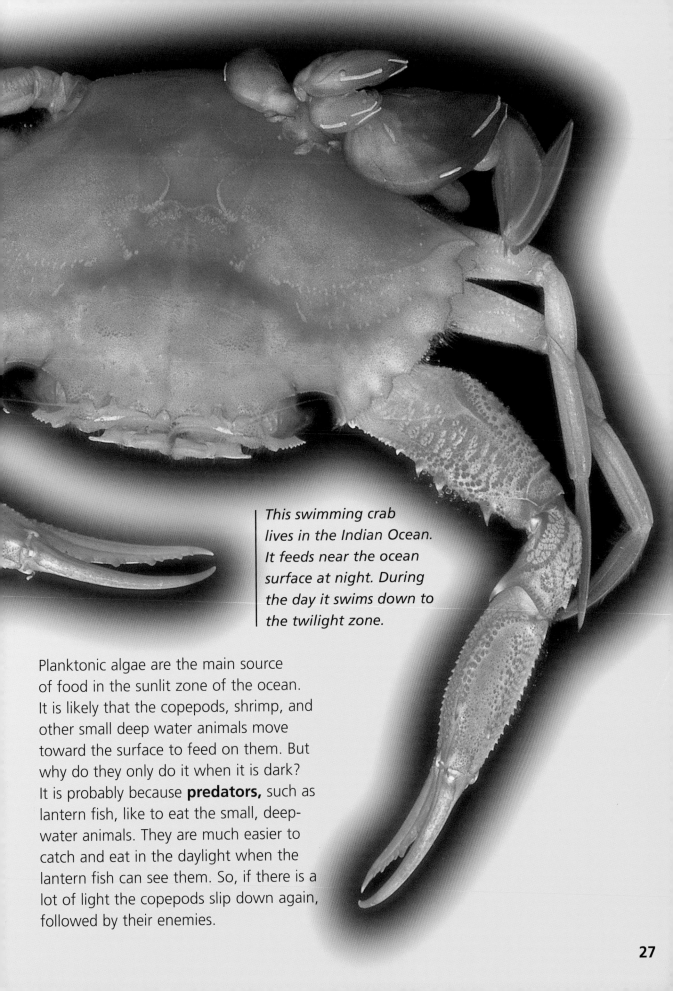

This swimming crab lives in the Indian Ocean. It feeds near the ocean surface at night. During the day it swims down to the twilight zone.

Planktonic algae are the main source of food in the sunlit zone of the ocean. It is likely that the copepods, shrimp, and other small deep water animals move toward the surface to feed on them. But why do they only do it when it is dark? It is probably because **predators,** such as lantern fish, like to eat the small, deep-water animals. They are much easier to catch and eat in the daylight when the lantern fish can see them. So, if there is a lot of light the copepods slip down again, followed by their enemies.

Big-Eyed Hunters

When you sampled the small animals in the **deep scattering layer,** you also caught some of the bigger ones. The catch included many squid, which are fast-swimming relatives of octopuses. There were also **streamlined** lantern fish and flattened, silvery hatchet fish. And there were various kinds of jellyfish and comb jellies.

eye ────────

Most of these animals move up and down in the water. They do this to keep track of smaller animals like copepods and shrimp, which they hunt for food. Some, such as jellyfish, rely on trapping prey in their trailing, stinging tentacles. The comb jellies are more active. They suck their victims into their hollow bodies. However, neither of these creatures has eyes, so they cannot see their prey.

Hunting outlines

By contrast, most of the deep water fish and squid that you've hauled up on deck have very big eyes. Big eyes work much better in dim light than small eyes. Big-eyed fish and squid are well equipped for hunting in the twilight zone.

The odd-looking hatchet fish is even better at seeing in poor light. It looks strange because its eyes are in an unusual place. Instead of looking sideways or forward, they look straight up from the top of its head. This allows it to peer up through the water.

Big eyes

Like peoples' eyes, those of a fish or squid work by gathering light through a see-through **lens.** The lens **focuses** the light to form an **image** on a sheet of light sensors. A small lens gathers less light than a big one, so it forms a dimmer image. If there is not much light, the lens may not form an image at all. So, animals that hunt by sight in the dark have very big eyes, with extra large lenses.

feeding
tentacle

arm

*Deep-water squid like this one have large
eyes so they can see the animals they hunt.*

Why is this helpful? Animals in the twilight
zone show up as black shapes (silhouettes)
against the faint light shining down from
above. If a **predator,** such as a hatchet
fish, can see its **prey** from below it can
snap them up.

*The mouth and eyes of a hatchet fish face
up from the top of its head. This allows the
fish to look up and eat animals above it.*

Top Predators

The fish and squid that eat the copepods and other small animals have enemies of their own. Plenty of bigger killers, such as sharks and large squid, patrol the twilight zone. They follow their **prey** toward the surface at night. They are joined by other hunters that spend most of their lives near the surface.

Your chances of seeing any of these big **predators** are not very good. Big hunters are always fewer in number than the animals that they eat. Most of them are also fast swimmers that cover large areas of ocean. But if you are in the right place at the right time, you might be lucky.

Surprise attack

You decide to keep the **ROV** operating below the boat, just in case. You switch on all the lights, so you do not miss anything. And you wait.

Two hours later, you are still waiting. It is 1 o'clock in the morning, and you are just thinking about giving up when a sleek shape appears. It is a blue shark. All sharks have an amazingly good sense of smell. Finding prey in the dark is no problem for them. The blue shark is different than most sharks. It often hunts in the twilight zone or even deeper in the ocean. But at night, it hunts nearer the surface.

The blue shark's favorite prey are squid. The shark you spotted has found a shoal of squid that has risen from the twilight zone to feed on small fish. The shark plunges into the shoal. It seizes the slippery squid with its sharp, hooked teeth. The squid are easy targets for the shark because they are lit up by ROV's lights.

You are so busy following the shark with the ROV camera that you almost miss another big hunter. At first you think it is another shark. Then, it comes within range of the lights and you see it has a long, sharp bill. It is a billfish called a marlin. As it passes you, it suddenly starts to swim faster, and it shoots away. Marlins can swim as fast as a cruising automobile drives along a highway. Since it is one of the fastest fish in the ocean, you were lucky to see it at all.

This blue shark in the sunlit zone is on the lookout for squid, its favorite food. Blue sharks are equally at home in the colder, darker waters of the twilight zone.

Mirrors and Light

You want to dive down among the animals of the **deep scattering layer** and see them for yourself. It is far too deep for normal diving, but luckily the Australian Navy can let you borrow an experimental pressure-proof suit. It can be used at 1,000 feet (300 meters). There is just one problem. The suit has no lights.

You decide to try it anyway. Many of the animals are **luminous,** so you should be able to see some of them in the dark. But you take a flashlight as well.

You dive before dawn, to get among the animals before they sink too deep. But when you get down to the right depth you cannot see much. By this time the sun has risen. The water is lit up with a faint blue glow. You look all around. There are no animals to see. Then you switch on the flashlight, and there are hatchet fish and lantern fish all around you. Why couldn't you see them before?

As you move close to a hatchet fish, its silver side reflects your flashlight like a mirror. When you switch the light off, the "mirror" reflects the blue glow from the surface. So the fish looks like the water around it. It is a bit like the office buildings covered in mirror glass that reflect the sky. They look like the sky themselves.

There is something else. When you look up at the fish from underneath, you still cannot see it very well. The fish should be a dark silhouette against the blue glow. But the luminous **organs** along its belly produce a blue light that exactly matches the glow in the water. So instead of making the fish easy to see, its lights actually help hide the fish.

If you were a hunter like the blue shark, you might have real trouble finding these fish. Their mirrors and lights act as camouflage that can make them almost impossible to see.

*Anglerfish (left) are named for the rod sticking out from their head. At the end of the rod is a **bioluminescent** organ.*

Liocranchia (right) is a deep-sea squid with bioluminescent eyes.

Bioluminescence

When light is created, heat is usually produced as well. But the light organs of fish make light without heat. They work by mixing special chemicals with oxygen. If the fish shuts off the oxygen supply, the lights go out. Light produced by living creatures is called bioluminescence.

Deep-Water Giants

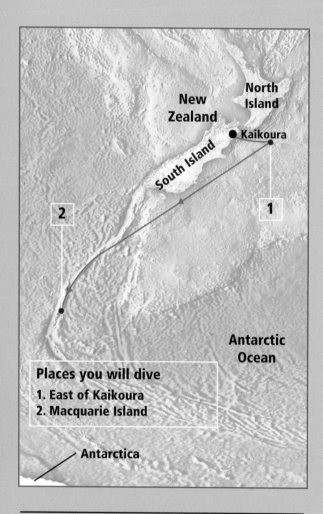

New Zealand

North Island

Kaikoura

South Island

2

1

Antarctic Ocean

Places you will dive
1. East of Kaikoura
2. Macquarie Island

Antarctica

No one has ever seen a giant squid alive. This is what people think one would look like as it swims. The human diver looks tiny in comparison.

The next stop on your ocean trip is Kaikoura in South Island, New Zealand. This place is on the edge of the South Pacific. The water here is rich in **plankton,** fish, and squid. These **organisms** attract huge whales such as sperm whales and humpback whales. You are going to dive with sperm whales.

A sperm whale can grow to 60 feet (18 meters) long. And it can weigh 50 tons (51 metric tons)—as heavy as 30 cars. A sperm whale's huge head takes up almost a third of its length. The whale dives into the twilight zone to feed on squid and fish. A sperm whale may stay underwater for an hour or more. Yet, like all whales, it breathes air. How does it do it?

A sperm whale stores lots of oxygen in its blood and muscles. While the whale is underwater, the oxygen is released to keep the heart and brain working. Its other **organs** probably stop working altogether. This allows the whale to stay underwater for longer. When it gets back to the surface, it can breathe fresh air again.

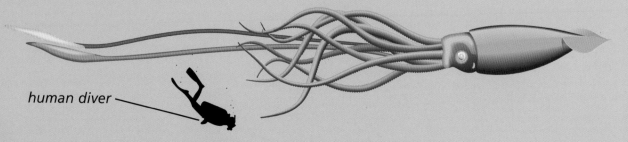

human diver

Sperm whales breathe in air at the ocean surface. Then they dive very deep in search of food to eat.

Diving for squid

You cannot dive into the twilight zone without help, like a sperm whale can. You have to follow it down in a **submersible.** You are lowered over the side of the ship near a whale with a big notch in its tail. The shape of its tail will keep you from confusing this whale with any other whales. Within a few minutes, the whale flips up its tail and dives under the surface.

The whale dives fast, because it wants to go deep. Your submersible can barely keep track of it. The whale goes down and down, into the gloom. It is searching for food. You are hoping to see it tangle with its favorite **prey**— a giant squid.

An epic struggle

No one has seen a giant squid alive. But we know they live in the ocean since dead ones sometimes get washed up on beaches. A giant squid can be almost as long as a sperm whale. Some sperm whales carry scars left by the suckers on giant squid tentacles. Giant squid use their tentacles to fight off the whales. You may get to watch a battle.

Talking Whales

Safe in your **submersible,** you follow the sperm whale down to the bottom of the twilight zone. As you watch, the whale chases after a group of squid. But although the squid are big, they are not giants. The whale seizes them with the large teeth in its long, narrow lower jaw. Then, it gulps them down.

The sperm whale turns and swims off. It is too fast for you to follow. Your lights can just pick out a pale shape in the water beyond the whale. Is it a giant squid? You try to get closer, but it is no use. You lose sight of both animals in the gloom. You will never know what the second animal was.

Clicking calls

There is another way you can keep track of the whale. You can follow the sounds it makes. Sperm whales can "talk" to each other using clicking sounds. The sounds can travel a long way through the water.

Social bonds between sperm whales are strong and long lasting. By calling to each other, mothers can look after their young, and a whale pod (group) can stay together.

In the depths of the twilight zone, a whale can hear the clicks being made by another whale at least 115 miles (185 kilometers) away. It would take a car almost two hours to drive that far on a highway.

You switch on an instrument called a **hydrophone.** You listen to the sounds coming out of it. There are lots of rasping noises. When you play them through the

Hydrophone

Your submersible is equipped with a hydrophone. This is a special type of **microphone** for listening underwater. It cannot hear sounds as well as a whale's ears can. But it can still pick up the clicks of a whale more than 6 miles (10 kilometers) away.

submersible's computer, it shows that the noises are fast bursts of clicks. Each burst has the same pattern. It is like some kind of sound code. The sounds seem to be coming from the whale that you were following. There are other clicks all around you, so there must be several sperm whales hunting down here. The coded clicks may mean something. Maybe the whale is telling the others that it has caught a giant squid! The whale is also using sound as **sonar,** like the ship that found the **deep scattering layer.** By listening to the echoes of its clicking calls, the whale can find squid and fish to eat. This is how it finds its **prey** even where there is very little light, at the bottom of the twilight zone.

Heading South

In spring, the big male sperm whales living in the southern oceans head farther south. They swim to the rich water around Antarctica. North of the **equator,** the males head north toward the Arctic Ocean. The smaller females and their young stay in warmer oceans all year.

Sperm whales are the only kind of whales that live like this. Other whales, such as humpbacks, travel in families. They feed in polar oceans in summer. In fall they swim to warmer water. But adult male and female sperm whales live apart for much of the year.

A team of scientists has attached a **satellite tracking device** to a whale so they can follow it underwater. You join the scientists as they follow the whale south. The sperm whale drives itself along using the broad, flat flukes of its tail. Every time it lifts its tail, it surges forward. When it lowers its tail, the flukes bend upward to spill the water. It swims about twice as fast as the speed you walk to school. It is heading for the area around Antarctica, where the **sea ice** is melting.

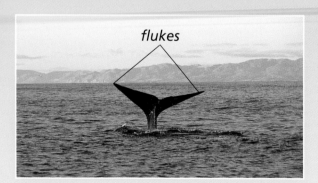

flukes

This sperm whale has come to the surface for air. Now it is diving again. Its tail flukes drive it forward when it is swimming.

Satellite tracking

A satellite tracking device is attached to an animal. The device makes contact with GPS navigation satellites (right) orbiting Earth. The system gives the exact place where the animal is. That location is then sent to the scientists operating the tracking device.

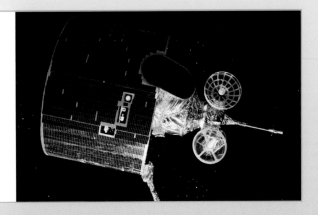

*A krill magnified around 10 times its real length under a **microscope**. In the ocean around Antarctica, penguins, seals, squid, and fish eat thousands of krill every day.*

Sea ice is frozen water that forms at the top of the sunlit zone in very cold places. When the sea ice melts, the sun shines on the surface water. This makes the **algae** in the **plankton** grow very fast. And this attracts huge swarms of shrimplike creatures called **krill.** They are eaten by fish, squid, seals, penguins, and whales. The whale is hunting the fish and squid.

Krill behave just like small animals in warmer oceans. They come near the surface at night and dive deep by day. Summer days are very long near the Antarctic, so the krill spend most of their time deep in the twilight zone. So do the fish and squid that eat them. The whale has to do the same to catch enough food.

Deep Currents

As you travel south after the sperm whale, you take the temperature of the ocean water. As you might expect, the surface water gets colder as you get near Antarctica. And the water in the twilight zone is much colder. It is also more salty. Why is that?

When salty seawater freezes at the surface in the polar oceans, it forms pure ice with no salt in it.

A scientist checks how salty the water is at the ocean surface near Antarctica.

Polar explorers can melt the ice and drink it. All the salt is left behind in the water below the ice. That makes the water below the ice saltier than normal. The water below the ice is also very cold.

Cold water is heavier than warmer water. Extra salt also makes water heavier. So the very cold, extra-salty water below the ice is unusually heavy. It sinks slowly toward the seafloor. As the very cold water sinks, it pushes away the cold, salty water that is already there. This cold bottom water then flows along the ocean floor. It forms a slow **current** that moves all the time. It is called the **ocean conveyor belt.**

Vital supplies

Part of the ocean conveyor belt flows north past New Zealand, and up into the Pacific Ocean. This was the water that you sampled on your journey south.

The current carries cold polar water toward the **equator.** It has a slight cooling effect on the **tropical** oceans.

The current flowing past New Zealand also contains a lot of nutrients scooped up from the ocean floor. It carries the nutrients north, too. Eventually, the nutrients fuel a rich growth of **plankton** in the northern Pacific Ocean. So, the whales that feed off Alaska can get more food because of a current that starts on the other side of Earth.

The animals that live in the twilight zone also gain. Water near the surface that is almost freezing **absorbs** a lot of oxygen from the air. As it sinks, the water carries this oxygen into the twilight zone. Without oxygen, animals could not live in the twilight zone or below. So without the ocean conveyor belt, the deep oceans would be completely dead.

Diving with Elephant Seals

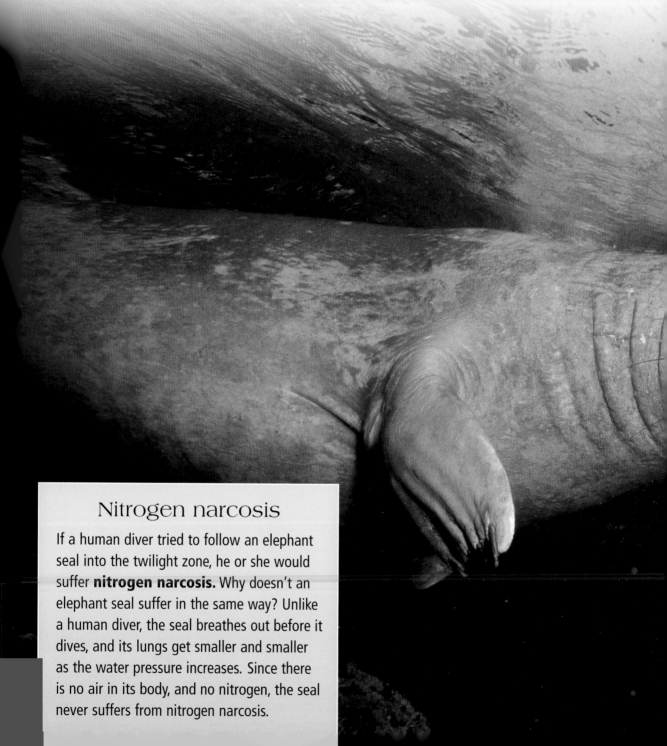

Nitrogen narcosis

If a human diver tried to follow an elephant
seal into the twilight zone, he or she would
suffer **nitrogen narcosis.** Why doesn't an
elephant seal suffer in the same way? Unlike
a human diver, the seal breathes out before it
dives, and its lungs get smaller and smaller
as the water pressure increases. Since there
is no air in its body, and no nitrogen, the seal
never suffers from nitrogen narcosis.

Next, you go to Macquarie Island, which is between New Zealand and Antarctica. There, you get a chance to meet another deep diver.

Macquarie Island is a breeding site for elephant seals. They are named for the trunklike nose and huge size of the males.

Elephant seals swim very well underwater. They can also dive to great depths. Some dive right through the twilight zone and into the midnight zone below.

Researchers have fitted some of the seals with **satellite tracking devices.** Each tracker is glued to a seal's fur behind its neck. The tracker falls off after a few weeks. Before it does, it sends back details of where the seal goes. The tracker tells researchers where the seal goes, how deep it dives, and how long it stays underwater.

You get to watch as the scientists track a hunting seal. The results are amazing. The seal spends nearly all its time underwater, even though it has to breathe air. When it dives, it plunges right down into the twilight zone, 1,300 feet (400 meters) or more. Elephant seals often stay underwater for half an hour. Some have been known to dive to 5,600 feet (1,700 meters), and stay under for two hours. That is twice as long as a basketball game.

Unlike a sperm whale, an elephant seal breathes out before it dives. That means the seal does not have any air in its body. This is very important because it means the seal does not suffer from nitrogen narcosis. The seal has to rely on oxygen stored in its blood and muscles. Its body processes slow down when it dives. Its heartbeat might slow to six beats a minute. Your heart beats more than 10 times as fast. A slower heartbeat reduces the amount of oxygen the seal needs.

Most animals that allow their bodies to slow down this much are in some kind of deep sleep. But the elephant seal stays active and alert. It can hunt and catch fish and squid, even deep in the mysterious world of the twilight zone.

Mission Debriefing

Your mission to the twilight zone has taught you a lot. You probably already guessed that it is cold and dark. Now you know exactly what this means for the animals that live there.

You discovered how the smallest animals feed on bits of dead plants and animals drifting down from above. And you saw how they migrate toward the surface every night to get a taste of something fresh. They are followed by crowds of hungry hunters in the greatest mass movement of animals on Earth.

You watched how some of these animals manage to find their prey. And you saw how others use tricks of the light to avoid being seen and eaten. You followed two air-breathing animals that have found ways of diving to the twilight zone in search of food. These animals were sperm whales and elephant seals. And you may have seen a giant squid —a true ocean monster.

Yet animals are only part of the story. On your journey you also discovered strange things like **thermoclines,** the **oxygen minimum layer,** and the **ocean conveyor belt.** They are all part of the unfamiliar world of the twilight zone.

This small creature lives in the twilight zone. It is called an amphipod, and it is part of the plankton.

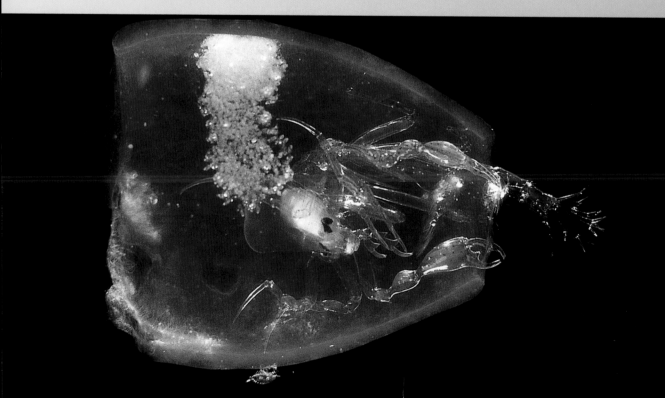

Glossary

absorb soak up

algae plantlike living things. Some are tiny, and others are big, like some seaweeds. Algae have no roots, stems, or leaves.

antennae feelers of organisms such as insects and copepods

bioluminescence light produced by living things

compressed air air that has been squeezed into a metal cylinder so it takes up less space

coral reef structure built by a large group of corals with chalky skeletons

current flow of ocean water

decompression chamber chamber where the air pressure can be changed. Divers enter the chamber so the air pressure on their bodies can be reduced slowly. This keeps them from becoming ill when they rise from deep water.

deep scattering layer layer of living things that spends the day in the twilight zone. It reflects or scatters sound.

dissolved mixed into a liquid

equator imaginary line around the center of Earth, halfway between the North and South Poles

feces pellets of animal waste

focus concentrate light rays to make a crisp, sharp picture

food chain links between living things that feed on each other

gills blood-filled organs that fish and other animals use to absorb oxygen from the water

hydrophone microphone designed to pick up sound signals underwater

image picture of something

insulation anything that keeps heat from passing from one place to another

krill shrimplike animals that live in huge swarms in the oceans around Antarctica

lens part of the eye that lets light through

luminous able to glow in the dark

magnify make something look bigger

marine snow tiny fragments of dead organisms that fall through the ocean

microscope tool for looking at things too small to see with the naked eye

mother ship ship that acts as a floating base for a submersible

nitrogen narcosis illness caused when nitrogen gas enters a diver's blood. It can happen when air in a diver's lungs is squeezed by the water pressure at great depths in the ocean.

ocean conveyor belt continuous ocean current that flows around Earth, mainly in the deep ocean

organic coming from living things

organisms living things. All plants and animals are organisms.

organs parts of living things with particular jobs to do. A heart is an organ. So are lungs.

oxygen minimum layer layer in the twilight zone where there is less oxygen than anywhere else

photosynthesis process by which plants use the Sun's energy to turn water and carbon dioxide into food

plankton community of organisms that drifts in the ocean, mainly near the surface

predators animals that hunt, kill, and eat other animals

prey animals that are killed and eaten by other animals

ROV (remotely operated vehicle) small underwater craft operated by remote control

satellite tracking device instruments that can be attached to animals. The devices beam information on the animals' location to satellites orbiting Earth. Then the information is sent to researchers.

scuba breathing apparatus used by divers

sea ice frozen part of the sunlit zone. Sea ice covers most of Arctic Ocean and the edges of Antarctica.

silhouetted seen as a dark shape against a lighter background

sonar method or device that locates things by finding reflected sound signals

streamlined smooth and rounded shape. Streamlined animals can move more easily through water or air.

submersible small submarine designed for short trips. Some can dive very deep.

the bends painful, dangerous condition suffered by divers who come to the surface too fast. It is caused by nitrogen bubbles in their blood.

thermocline boundary between two layers of water that have different temperatures

tropical warm. The very hot part of Earth on either side of the equator is tropical.

water pressure force of water pressing down on something

Further Reading and Websites

Books

Earle, Sylvia. *National Geographic Atlas of the Ocean: The Deep Frontier.* Washington, D.C.: National Geographic Society, 2001.

Kovacs, Deborah. *Dive to the Deep Ocean: Voyages of Exploration and Discovery.* Austin, Texas: Raintree, 1999.

Vogel, Carole G. *Underwater Exploration.* Danbury, Conn.: Franklin Watts, 2003.

Websites

www.bbc.co.uk/nature/blueplanet
The website of the BBC series about ocean life, with extra information and games.

oceanexplorer.noaa.gov
The website of the U.S. National Oceanic and Atmospheric Administration, about the technology of ocean exploration and ocean wildlife.

www.seasky.org/sea.html
A website packed with information about the ocean.

www.whalewatch.co.nz
The website of the Kaikoura whale-watching organization in New Zealand, with a lot of information on local whale sightings.

www.dal.ca/~ceph/TCP/vampy.html
Find out about the vampire squid, which spends its whole life in the oxygen minimum layer.

www.whalesongs.org/cetacean/ sperm_whales/home.html
Listen to the clicks and creaks of sperm whales.

Index